SECRETS OF CAVEMAN COOKING

FOR THE MODERN CAVEMAN

RECIPES FOR GRILLS & SMOKERS

BY RICK SNIDER

GOLDEN WEST☼ PUBLISHERS

Cover and text illustrations by Mike Obrenovich

DEDICATION

To my taste-testing daughters Katie and Megan,
who bravely tried some recipes; Roxie for eating the
scraps and my wife Lisa for being a good sport.

Printed in the United States of America

2nd printing © 2002

ISBN #1-885590-84-9

Golden West Publishers, Inc.
4113 N. Longview Ave.
Phoenix, AZ 85014, USA
(602) 265-4392

Visit our website: http://www.goldenwestpublishers.com

TABLE OF CONTENTS

BARBECUE SAUCES

BEEF

BURGERS

CHICKEN

PORK

LAMB

FISH & SEAFOOD

TABLE OF CONTENTS
(Continued)

CAVEMAN VERSUS MODERN MAN

Eating is our most primal urge. More than thirst. More than sex. More than money or power.

The caveman worried most over where his next meal would come from. He had to track it down, kill it and then eat it . . . raw! But, when that first bolt of lightning caught a tree on fire, man learned cooked food tasted a whole lot better.

So here we are 27,000 years after the first cooked caveman meals and we still like cooking outdoors. No pasta salads. No casseroles. No low-fat yogurt.

I'm talking caveman food. Ribs so big they'll flip Fred Flintstone's car over. Burgers that take two hands to eat. Steaks the size of a dictionary. Real man food. Caveman food.

We just can't get enough of that flame-broiled taste. Nearly three-fourths of U.S. households own a barbecue grill. That's 75 million households! They cook on them more than once per week with 58 percent owning charcoal grills and 59 percent owning gas grills. Obviously, some have both. Last year, 11.6 million grills and 864 thousand tons of charcoal were sold.

I'm not just talking summertime cookouts because 52 percent of Americans grill year-round. And when it comes to entertaining, 42 percent prefer barbecues to formal dining.

Mostly, barbecuing is a modern caveman, not cavewoman, thing by a 61-39 percent margin. Remember, Fred cooked bronto burgers on the grill while Wilma boiled eggs on the stove.

Now, there's no one way to barbecue. Indeed, there's more than one way to spell barbecue, like barbeque or BBQ. That's why our recipes can be used on both gas and charcoal grills.

You'll learn how to smoke a turkey, barbecue shrimp and cook chicken over a filled beer can. But let's go a step further. How about making pizza on a gas grill? What about a banana split?

(No, we don't put ice cream on the grates!) Enjoy grilled potatoes and corn in the husk. Try bean soup, cornbread, pancakes or omelets to name a few.

Modern cavemen can prepare an entire meal from soups to desserts right on their grills. If you can cook it on the stove or in an oven, you can prepare it on a grill or inside a smoker.

And you know one of the best parts (aside from the great taste) of cooking outdoors? A caveman's diet is better for you than modern menus. That's right, the caveman may not have lived as long as modern man, but he was a lot healthier before the dinosaurs ate him. I know, man and dinosaurs lived 60 million years apart, but work with me here.

According to *USA Weekend* magazine, a caveman's diet was 65 percent fruits, nuts and vegetables and 35 percent meat and seafood. Fifty-five percent of modern man's diet wasn't even available to cavemen, as we consume grains, milk, fat, alcohol and sweeteners. Modern man's diet includes only 17 percent fruits, nuts and vegetables and 28 percent meat and seafood. We're lacking in minerals and antioxidants, now usually consumed through supplements. No wonder modern man has diabetes, high blood pressure, heart disease and cancer, diseases that were rarely found in cavemen.

Let's get primal. Let's eat grilled salmon, smoked ham and barbecued shrimp. Chow down on seafood pizza, quesadillas, fajitas and sweet potatoes. I have included an Exotic Meats section that will tell you how to order and cook rare meats that will impress your neighbors.

However, beef and pork are still our favorite meats with chicken, turkey and fish becoming increasingly popular. The U.S. Department of Agriculture reports Americans eat 63.9 pounds of beef annually, 49.1 pounds of pork, 47.9 pounds of chicken, 14.3 pounds of turkey and 15 pounds of fish. That's why I offer recipes for all of them.

So grab your matches and head to the grill. It's time for some good eating!

Rick "The Caveman Cook" Snider

TOOLS OF THE TRADE

Gas versus Charcoal

This is like plastic versus paper. I don't take a stand on whether to use gas or charcoal grills. It's whatever you prefer. Gas is definitely faster and cleaner, but charcoal backers claim their method is tastier. All of the recipes in this book use a gas grill except for the Smoked Meats section.

Cavemen have usually been partial to fast food. If it takes longer to cook than to eat, some believe you're wasting your time. Then again, these are the same people who drive 90 miles per hour and always seem to be in a rush to get to who knows where. Many barbecuers like the slow lane and don't mind investing extra time because cooking is half the fun.

Why not use both grills? Indeed, a poll showed Americans are nearly evenly split, with gas grills found in 59 percent of households and charcoal grills in 58 percent. Obviously, some have both. Having both grills provides flexibility. You may prefer to use gas when cooking a couple of quick burgers on the grill. Charcoal could be used for roasting lamb chops.

Smokers

Getting serious, are you? The real caveman likes fire. Sure, gas grills are fast, clean and efficient, but so are car washes. The difference between gas grills and smokers is like a power car wash versus handwashing from a bucket in your driveway. The outcome is about the same, but the slower method can be more fun!

Now, cavemen aren't usually a patient group. They can't stand still for too long because they never know when a T-Rex will show up. They usually like everything quick (which also explains sex) as a safety precaution.

But let's say your cave is a safe haven and you have an afternoon to spend around the fire without having to constantly stir the pot. A smoker provides a slow, steady heat that deepens the flavor. Just don't check on it too often because it takes 15 minutes to restore maximum heat. Hourly basting is enough.

UTENSILS

Writers have their pencils, plumbers have their wrenches and cavemen have their own cooking utensils. A fork will do in a pinch, but let's look like a pro. First off, cavemen don't wear "kiss the cook" aprons or Pillsbury Dough Boy poofy hats. And don't even think about those oversized potholder gloves.

Spatulas are the most personalized hardware. They come long and thin or short and fat. Wide spatulas are stronger, thinner ones more flexible. Keep two so you'll always have one clean.

Tongs are worth spending a little extra on. Get heavyweight, long ones. The short ones can leave your hands burned.

Gloves are for sissies unless you're using a smoker or open pit. If you need gloves, buy fire-resistant ones. In fact, call your local firehouse and ask where they buy their gloves. Forget those kitchen ovenmitts that can catch fire.

Thermometers are an absolute necessity when cooking large meats like a turkey or roast. Be sure yours has a sharp point.

Skewers are great for kabobs. There are wooden and metal skewers. It's a matter of personal taste. Wooden skewers should be soaked for at least 20 minutes before using. Both must be cleaned after use.

Basting brushes apply your sauces like painting a canvas. Have two so you don't dip your brush in a competing flavor. It's like dipping a red brush in yellow paint.

Long-handled forks are great for lifting heavy items like roasts or whole chickens onto plates. A dinner fork can be used for flipping burgers if your spatula is dirty.

Cutting boards should be separated for meats and vegetables to avoid contamination. You absolutely must clean them afterwards to avoid food poisoning. Use an anti-bacterial cleanser because cutting boards aren't sterile just because they look clean.

A wire brush with stiff bristles for cleaning the metal grates is a must. Always clean the grates after cooking while they're still hot.

WOOD CHIPS

One of the best parts of cooking outdoors is the smell. You get hungry just catching a whiff of the grill. Your neighbors are suddenly wondering, what's for dinner?

Wood chips are a nice added touch, like whipped cream on strawberries. Your meat or fish will taste great anyway, but wood chips boost that woodsy or sweet flavor. It's like the difference between a Snickers bar and Godiva chocolate. Wood chips aren't noted in these recipes. I prefer to use them in smokers or charcoal grills, though you can use wood chips with gas grills in a metal smoke box or in a tin foil package with holes poked in it. Sold in many hardware stores or specialty shops, wood chips aren't that expensive. Usually $2 to $3 for a small bag. Soak the chips for 20 to 30 minutes in water before using or they'll flare out in seconds. Wet chips should be scattered over coals. A couple of handfuls are enough.

Wood chips are either smoky or sweet. It's better not to combine the tastes. Absolutely avoid any chips with chemicals or those coming from press-treated lumber or painted wood. Hickory and mesquite chips are the two most popular chips, according to a Barbecue Industry Association poll. Hickory is a traditional Southern barbecue flavor for beef and pork. Mesquite has gained favor in the past decade, but be careful to use it sparingly to avoid a bitter taste. It's also delicious with pork, beef and fish. Maple and oak also provide a woodsy taste. Maple works best with ham or turkey while oak is delicious with fowl. Try either with whole potatoes.

Have a sweet tooth? Sassafras is excellent with seafood. Apple works well with ham or pork. Cherry livens lamb or fowl. The trio intensify sweet potatoes.

Flavored charcoal is also starting to become a hit. You can find mesquite charcoal for about the same price as regular. A medium-sized bag is usually about $3 at grocery stores.

SAFETY TIPS

Cavemen are scared of fire. We wouldn't even come near fire if it didn't make food taste so much better. Read the grill owner's manual before using and keep the following safety tips in mind:

● Think of your LP-gas canisters like bombs because if they blow it will look like a bomb went off. Store them outdoors, in the shade, in an upright position. Not in a shed or garage, but where the vapors can be dissipated by the air. Don't store any combustible liquids nearby.

● Don't keep extra gas cylinders. Sure, you take a risk of running out of gas (it happens to us all), but an occasional check should be a proper reminder to refill it.

● Make sure the lid is open while lighting the burners. If you don't, you won't be around to make that mistake twice. If your first attempt at lighting fails and you smell gas, turn off the burners and wait five minutes before attempting to light again. A gas vapor buildup could cause a fireball. You'd look awfully funny without eyebrows. If several attempts to light the grill fail, turn off the burners and check the gas fittings. Do not use a match to search for leaks. Instead, spray soapy water on all fittings. Bubbles indicate a leak. Replace fitting before using grill.

● Don't use grills on wooden porches, balconies or beneath overhangs. The heat could cause a ceiling fire or at best blacken the paint and give you something else to do on the weekends.

● Be sure the grill is on an even surface. Otherwise, it could tip over and at best ruin the meal and at worst start a fire.

● Don't leave the grill unattended for more than a few minutes and never if children are nearby. Use discretion in regard to pets. My dog has never bothered my grills, but yours might knock it over.

● Turn off the LP-cylinder valve after use. Besides increased safety, it avoids waste from a slow leak.

● Dispose of dented or rusty gas cylinders through your local recycling program.

FEEDING THE CLAN

How Much is Enough?

When it comes to barbecuing, you can never make too much. There's something about the smell of outdoor cooking that turns otherwise normal people into grunting cavemen jumping around the fire. People eat at least twice as much as at normal meals. I've seen skinny people come back for thirds. Most barbecuers are known for letting out their belt a notch after a weekend foodfest.

Still, there has to be some idea of how much to cook when having people over. Here's a portion per person chart to be used as a guideline. When in doubt, make more. You can always use extras for leftovers, though we've seldom seen any.

Poultry
Chicken (boneless) ..... 1/2 pound
Chicken (parts) .... 2 pieces
Turkey .... 1 pound

Seafood
Fish fillets .... 6 ounces
Lobster (meat) .... 8 ounces
Lobster (shell) .... 2 pounds
Shrimp (peeled) .... 8 ounces

Beef
Hamburger .... 1/4 pound
Pot roast .... 1/2 pound
Rib roast .... 1/2 pound

Pork
Chops .... 2 large chops
Spareribs .... 1 pound
Roast .... 1/2 pound

Lamb
Leg .... 1/2 pound
Rack .... 4 ribs
Roast .... 4 ribs
Chops .... 2 large chops

HOW HOT IS HOT?

The rite of passage to manhood for some cavemen may have been killing dinner with a stick. Others saw visions in a smoky hut. In our cave (neighborhood), it was called "Brave Club" where you had to accept a dare from the elders (usually 13 to 18 year olds).

Like, how long could you hold your hand over the fire without screaming. This was a mandatory challenge around campfires. Who would have ever thought there was a practical side to it? This simple test, which depends on your pain threshold, tells how hot the grill is. If you can hold your hand over the grill:

1 second = 600 degrees or more
2 seconds = 500 degrees
3 seconds = 450 degrees
4 seconds = 400 degrees
5 seconds = 350 degrees
6 seconds = 300 degrees or less

What's so important about this test other than proving your "cavemanhood"? It's important to know the temperatures when cooking meats to determine their doneness. Now, anyone can tell when a hamburger is well done, but here's a guide on Fahrenheit temperatures for cooking meats using an instant-read meat ther- mometer.

Lamb
Rare—140 degrees
Medium—150 degrees
Well—170 degrees

Pork
Rare—Unsafe to eat
Medium—150 degrees
Well—160 degrees

Veal
Rare—Unsafe to eat
Medium—150 degrees
Well—160 degrees

Beef
Rare—125 degrees
Medium—155 degrees
Well—175 degrees

Poultry
Rare—Unsafe to eat
Medium—155 degrees
Well—165 degrees

Fish
Fish is done when opaque and flakes eas- ily with a fork.

BARBECUE SAUCES

Some believe the secret of great barbecue is the cooking method. Others believe it's the sauce. But not some sauce out of the bottle, a homemade version.

Many cavemen don't care whether it's a bottled sauce or something made in your bathtub. There are many great-tasting store-bought sauces, and I say use whatever you like and as much as you like. Store-bought sauces often have a lot of sugar that burns, so you might want to add them a few minutes before the meat is ready. However, I know fellow cavemen who marinate their meat with the sauce and then pour it atop during cooking.

If you'd like to make your own sauce, here are a few simple recipes. But one word of caution—you'll be fiddling with them the rest of your life. True barbecue sauce makers are always trying something different while guarding their secret sauces like Colonel Sanders protecting his seven secret herbs and spices.

Remember, when preparing a sauce or marinade that contains an acid ingredient (vinegar, lemon juice or wine), be sure to use a glass, ceramic or stainless steel container, never aluminum.

RIB SAUCE

1 cup tomato sauce
1 cup vinegar
1 cup water
2 tsp. salt
1 tbsp. butter

1 tsp. honey
dash of pepper

MAKES 3 CUPS

Combine all ingredients in a saucepan and mix thoroughly. Bring to a boil, then simmer for 15 minutes. Place in a bowl, cover and cool for several hours until thickened.

THREE-ALARM SAUCE

1 tbsp. onion flakes
1 tbsp. salt
3 tsp. hot pepper sauce
3 tsp. sugar
1 pint cider vinegar

MAKES 1 PINT

Combine all ingredients in a mixing bowl, pouring in the vinegar last. Mix well. Let stand 3 hours.

SWEET SAUCE

2 cups ketchup
2 cups sugar
1/2 cup water
1 cup lemon juice
3 tsp. butter
2 tsp. molasses
1 tsp. honey
1 tsp. hot sauce
1 tsp. steak sauce

MAKES 3 CUPS

Combine all ingredients in a saucepan and mix thoroughly. Bring to a boil, then simmer for 15 minutes. Place in a bowl, cover and let cool for several hours until thickened.

REFRIGERATOR DOOR SAUCE

12 ounces ketchup
1/4 cup honey
1/4 cup mustard
2 tsp. sherry vinegar
2 tbsp. water
1 tbsp. Worcestershire sauce
1 tsp. olive oil

MAKES 1 1/2 CUPS

Combine all ingredients in a saucepan and mix thoroughly. Bring to a boil, then simmer for 15 minutes. Place in a bowl, cover and let cool for several hours until thickened.

SPICY TOMATO SAUCE

1 cup spicy tomato juice
1/3 cup hoisin sauce
3 tbsp. orange juice
2 tbsp. water
1 tsp. olive oil
1 tsp. lemon juice
1 tsp. chopped onion

MAKES 1 1/2 CUPS

Combine all ingredients in a saucepan and mix thoroughly. Bring to a boil, then simmer for 15 minutes. Place in a bowl, cover and cool for several hours until thickened.

BEEF

RUSTLER T-BONES

As a teenager, I cooked at a now-closed chain of Rustler steak houses. You could get a complete T-bone steak dinner for just $1.99, and the line of hungry diners literally snaked outside the building. My 12-foot-long broiler would be filled with dozens of T-bone steaks while serving more than 200 people per hour. (No wonder I would talk in my sleep saying, "Throw more bones on the grill.") And, brother cavemen, they were the best T-bones I ever ate!

> 4 (1 pound) T-bone steaks
> 1 cup barbecue sauce (see pages 13-15)
> salt and pepper to taste

1. Preheat gas grill for 10 minutes with burners on high.

2. Baste your T-bones with your favorite barbecue sauce. However, go lightly because T-bones are so tasty that you don't want to mask the flavor with sauce.

3. Turn burners to low and place T-bones on grill. Close grill lid. You don't want to burn the meat, but slowly simmer it. Cook 3 minutes per side for rare, 6 minutes for medium and 8 minutes for well done.

Serves:

Filet Mignon

You're going to have to be a patient caveman to eat one of these prime cuts of beef. You could use the smoker to cook it, though it would take more than one hour. The key is to not burn the filet, but let it cook slowly so the outside doesn't burn while the inside stays raw. The extra few minutes are well worth the wait!

4 (1 pound) filets, at least 1-inch thick

Basting Sauce:
  1/2 cup olive oil
  1/2 cup lemon juice
  1/2 cup dry sherry
  1/2 tsp. ground black pepper
  1 tsp. minced onion flakes

1. Preheat gas grill for 10 minutes with burners on high.

2. Mix ingredients in bowl and baste filets.

3. Turn burners to low and place filets on grill. Close grill lid. Cook 5 minutes per side for rare, 9 minutes for medium and 12 minutes for well done.

Note: To increase cooking speed, use a butterfly cut (slice midway through the filet) and spread meat open over grill.

Serves:

NEW YORK STRIP

Some people love T-bones, filet mignon or porterhouses, but ounce for ounce, a New York strip is unbeatable. It's the working caveman's best value, too!

4 (8 ounce) strip steaks

Marinade:
- **1 cup water**
- **1/4 cup minced green bell pepper**
- **1 tbsp. virgin olive oil**
- **1 tbsp. ground black pepper**
- **1 tbsp. minced onion**

1. Combine marinade ingredients and pour over steak. This gives it a slight flavor, but New York strip is so tasty, you don't want to mask the natural flavor. Refrigerate for 30 minutes.

2. Preheat gas grill for 10 minutes with burners on high.

3. Turn burners to low and place steaks on grill. Close grill lid. Cook steaks 5 minutes per side for rare, 9 minutes for medium and 12 minutes for well done.

Serves:

GRILLED SIRLOIN WITH ORANGE MARINADE

A true caveman never tires of beef, but even serious barbarians like something different once in a while. This will give you a taste of the tropics!

2 (1 pound) sirloin steaks (fat removed)

Marinade:
    1 cup strained orange juice
    1/2 cup balsamic vinegar
    2 tsp. orange zest
    1 tsp. black pepper
    1 small onion, minced

1. Mix ingredients for marinade. Pour over steaks and marinate in refrigerator for 30 minutes.

2. Preheat gas grill for 10 minutes with burners on high.

3. Turn burners to medium. Place steaks on grill reserving marinade. Close grill lid. Cook 3 to 6 minutes per side, depending on preferred doneness. Baste with remaining marinade when flipping.

Serves:

Flank Steaks with Rum

While working in the Dominican Republic, there was a big opening-day bash for the company's new racetrack. Chicken is the most commonplace meat, so having steak was a treat for the locals. Everyone ate and drank and the party really flowed. I thought these Caribbean cavemen really knew how to party. Turns out the steak was marinated in rum and the "Presidente" beer was four times stronger than American beer. We slept well that night!

4 (8 ounce) flank steaks

Marinade:
- **2 cups rum**
- **2 cups water**
- **2 tbsp. black molasses**
- **2 tbsp. brown sugar**
- **2 tbsp. honey**

1. Mix marinade ingredients in a bowl and pour over steaks. Marinate in refrigerator for one hour.

2. Preheat gas grill for 10 minutes with burners on high.

3. Turn burners to medium and place steaks on grill reserving marinade. Close grill lid. Cook 3 minutes per side for rare, 5 minutes for medium and 8 minutes for well done. Baste with remaining marinade when flipping.

Note: Obviously, this isn't a recipe for underage folks.

Serves:

BURGERS

BACON CHEESEBURGERS

Anyone can just put the toppings on a burger. Let's include them inside the meat. When you get to the cheesy bacon middle, it is pure nirvana!

2 pounds lean hamburger
8 slices precooked bacon
1 cup shredded cheese
salt and pepper to taste

1. Preheat gas grill for 10 minutes with burners on high.

2. Make 8 burgers that are thin and wide. Place a slice of bacon in the center of each burger and sprinkle with cheese; add salt and pepper. Fold edges in to seal the center.

3. Turn burners to medium. While it seems ironic to use lean hamburger, it has less fat so the drippings don't increase the flames and burn the meat.

4. Place burgers on grill. Close grill lid. Cook 3 minutes per side for rare, 5 minutes for medium and 7 minutes for well done. Remember, they'll take a little longer than usual because they're thicker.

5. Don't forget to toast the buns on the grill!

Serves:

TURKEY BURGERS

Love burgers on the grill but can't handle the grease or cholesterol? Ground turkey has become the hottest trend for health-conscious cavemen. It needs a little flavoring help, but that's what barbecuing is all about anyway!

> **1 1/2 pounds ground turkey**
> **salt and pepper to taste**
> **1 cup barbecue sauce (see pages 13-15)**

1. Preheat gas grill for 10 minutes with burners on high.

2. Mix salt and pepper and your favorite barbecue sauce into the meat. Make 4 burgers.

3. Turn burners to medium. Baste tops of burgers with sauce.

4. Place burgers on grill. Close grill lid. Cook 3 minutes per side for rare, 6 minutes for medium and 8 minutes for well done. Be sure to baste after flipping.

5. Don't forget to toast the buns on the grill!

Serves:

VENISON-PORK CHEESEBURGERS

Two passions of caveman cooks are venison and pork.
So, why not combine both for a hearty cheeseburger?

1 pound ground venison
1/2 pound ground pork
1 cup shredded cheese
1 tbsp. minced onion
1 tbsp. ground black pepper
1 tsp. oregano

1. Preheat gas grill for 10 minutes with burners on high.

2. Combine all ingredients and make 4 burgers.

3. Turn burners to medium and place burgers on grill. Close grill lid. Cook 4 minutes per side for rare, 7 minutes for medium and 9 minutes for well done.

4. Don't forget to toast the buns on the grill!

Serves:

Moose Burgers

OK, I could call them "Bullwinkle Burgers" but this sounds more cavemanly. If you ever bag a moose, you'll be eating moose burgers from Memorial Day to Labor Day!

2 pounds ground moose
1 pound lean hamburger

Seasoning:
    2 tbsp. minced onion
    2 tbsp. fresh ground pepper
    2 tsp. Worcestershire sauce
    1 tsp. soy sauce

1. Preheat gas grill for 10 minutes with burners on high.

2. Mix meat and seasoning ingredients together in a bowl and make 8 burgers.

3. Turn burners to medium and place burgers on grill. Close grill lid. Cook 4 minutes per side for rare, 7 minutes for medium and 9 minutes for well done.

4. Don't forget to toast the buns on the grill!

Serves:

CHICKEN

CHICKEN PARMESAN

Cavemen love cheese. You'll save it for last, but cheese really awakens the flavor of chicken!

4 chicken breasts
4 chicken parts

Basting Sauce:
   1/2 cup olive oil
   2 tsp. oregano
   1 tsp. minced onion
   4 tsp. Parmesan cheese

1/2 cup shredded cheese

1. Preheat gas grill for 10 minutes with burners on high.

2. Mix oil, oregano, onion and Parmesan cheese in a bowl. Baste chicken with mixture, saving remainder for later.

3. Turn burners to medium and place chicken on grill. Close grill lid. Cook 8 minutes per side for breasts, 6 minutes for parts. Baste chicken after flipping.

4. After removing from grill, sprinkle shredded cheese atop chicken and let melt before serving.

Serves:

Honey Barbecued Chicken

A classic. Indoor cooks may consider fried chicken the staple of Sunday dinners, but caveman cooks know barbecued chicken is far tastier!

4 chicken breasts
4 chicken parts (legs, wings)

Basting Sauce:
    1 1/2 cups barbecue sauce (see pages 13-15)
    1 cup honey
    2 tbsp. molasses
    2 tbsp. olive oil

1. Preheat gas grill for 10 minutes with burners on high.

2. Mix basting ingredients in a small saucepan. Warm slightly so honey and molasses jell with sauce. Baste chicken with sauce and save remainder for later.

3. Turn burners to medium and place chicken on grill. Close grill lid. Cook 8 minutes per side for breasts, 6 minutes for parts. Baste chicken after flipping.

4. After removing from grill, baste once more before serving.

Serves:

BEER-CAN CHICKEN

Many barbecuers drink beer while cooking. Why not combine the taste of both? Non-drinkers can even use the non-alcoholic beers. Just remember, no fancy imported beers. Any domestic brew will do!

1 whole chicken
3/4 cup barbecue sauce
 (see pages 13-15)
1 (12 ounce) can of beer

1. Preheat gas grill for 10 minutes with burners on high.

2. Clean chicken under cold running water. Baste chicken with barbecue sauce.

3. Cut off the top of the beer can using a can opener. Place cavity of chicken over can (with beer still inside, get another one if you're thirsty) leaving only 1 or 2 inches of can showing. Sit can atop grill so it's balanced upright. Close grill lid.

4. Cook for approximately 30 minutes. When chicken becomes so tender it falls off the can, it should be ready. However, inspect for doneness. If not thoroughly cooked, cut chicken in half and continue cooking.

Serves:

CHICKEN FRUIT KABOBS

Chicken and fruit are staples of tropical island cavemen. They love smothering meats with pineapples and mangoes. It certainly makes for sweet mouth-watering eating!

4 deboned chicken breasts
24 one-inch thick pineapple cubes
24 one-inch thick apple cubes
24 one-inch thick mango cubes
24 one-inch thick apricot cubes

1. Preheat gas grill for 10 minutes with burners on high.

2. Slice chicken into 24 pieces.

3. Place chicken and fruits on skewers (if using wooden skewers, soak for 20 minutes before using). Alternate in any pattern, but best to have pineapple beside chicken.

4. Turn burners to medium and place skewers on grill. Close grill lid. Cook 5 minutes per side.

5. Remove from skewers and serve.

Serves:

CHICKEN VEGETABLE KABOBS

Vegetarians and meat-loving cavemen unite for this dish. You get the healthy benefit of eating vegetables and non-red meat, though cavemen barbecuers traditionally love red meat. This is a chance to impress fellow cavemen with a "classy dish!"

4 deboned chicken breasts
24 cherry tomatoes
6 small onions
3 green bell peppers
3 lemons

1. Preheat gas grill for 10 minutes with burners on high.

2. Slice chicken into 24 pieces. Quarter onions. Cut green bell peppers and lemons into eighths.

3. Place chicken and vegetables on skewers (if using wooden skewers, soak for 20 minutes before using). Alternate in any pattern, but best to have peppers beside chicken.

4. Turn burners to medium and place skewers on grill. Close grill lid. Cook 5 minutes per side.

5. Remove from skewers and serve.

Serves:

CHICKEN, BEANS & BISCUITS

A hearty trail food. Cowboy cavemen have been eating biscuits and beans beside campfires for more than a century. Let's make it even more tasty with chicken!

4 **chicken breasts**
1 **cup barbecue sauce (see pages 13-15)**
1 **(16 ounce) can baked beans**
1 **cup water**
4 **biscuits**
1 **tbsp. cinnamon**

1. Preheat gas grill for 10 minutes with burners on high.

2. Debone chicken into filets. Baste with barbecue sauce.

3. Turn burners on one side to medium and place chicken on that side of the grill. Cook 5 minutes per side. Leave lid open.

4. Using a cast-iron skillet, mix beans and water and cook on the side of grill with burners on high. By the time the chicken is ready, the beans will be hot.

5. When chicken is done, remove and cut into bite-size pieces. Add chicken to the beans and turn burners to low setting. Crumble and stir biscuits into beans. Cook for 5 minutes.

6. Remove skillet from grill and let cool for 2 minutes. Sprinkle cinnamon across top.

Serves:

LEMON CHICKEN

This isn't like the Chinese dish served with rice, though you can serve it that way if you want. The lemon flavor here is more understated and not a sauce. It will make your mouth curl in delight!

4 chicken breasts
4 chicken parts

Basting Sauce:
   1 cup virgin olive oil
   1 tbsp. ground pepper
   juice of 2 lemons

1. Preheat gas grill for 10 minutes with burners on high.

2. Mix oil, pepper and lemon juice in a bowl. Baste chicken.

3. Turn burners to medium and place chicken on grill. Close grill lid. Cook 8 minutes per side, basting after flipping.

Serves:

PORK

YABBA-DABBA-DO RIBS

Remember the end of the Flintstones cartoon when Fred would order ribs so big they would flip the car? I haven't been able to find any that size, but there's nothing better than gorging on ribs!

6 pounds pork ribs

Marinade:
- **1 cup melted butter**
- **1/2 cup water**
- **1/4 cup minced green bell pepper**
- **1/4 cup minced onion**
- **2 tbsp. ground black pepper**
- **1 tbsp. olive oil**
- **1 tsp. cayenne pepper**
- **1 tsp. coarse salt**

1. Mix marinade ingredients in a bowl and pour over ribs which have been sliced into single ribs. Marinate in refrigerator for 30 minutes.

2. Preheat gas grill for 10 minutes with burners on high.

3. Turn burners to medium and place ribs on grill reserving marinade. Close grill lid. Cook 10 minutes per side for well done. Remember, do not eat pink pork. Be sure to baste ribs with remaining marinade after turning.

Serves:

TROPICAL PORK CHOPS

Pork lends itself to the sweetest tasting recipes. I love this honey and pineapple combination—serve it at any party!

8 (6 ounce) pork chops

Marinade:
    1/4 cup olive oil
    8 tsp. honey
    4 tsp. black molasses
    2 tbsp. soy sauce
    2 tbsp. cinnamon
    2 tsp. ginger

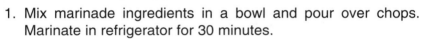

1 cored pineapple

1. Mix marinade ingredients in a bowl and pour over chops. Marinate in refrigerator for 30 minutes.

2. Preheat gas grill for 10 minutes with burners on high.

3. Turn burners to medium and place chops on grill reserving marinade. Close grill lid. Cook 8 minutes per side for medium and 10 minutes for well done. Remember, do not eat pink pork. Be sure to baste with marinade after turning.

4. Slice pineapple and cut into small cubes. Serve over pork.

Serves:

Cajun Ribs

First, get a big glass of ice water and set it next to your plate with a filled pitcher nearby. You're going to need it because the Cajun cavemen don't play around when cooking. Their idea of mild is often considered hot by most standards. They like to laugh at visitors whose faces turn bright red. Still, if you can stand the heat, it's worth hanging around the kitchen for these ribs!

6 pounds pork ribs

Marinade:
- **1 cup tomato purée**
- **1/4 cup chopped onion**
- **1/4 cup chopped garlic cloves**
- **2 tbsp. chili powder**
- **1 tbsp. lemon juice**
- **1 tbsp. Tabasco® sauce**
- **1 tsp. butter**
- **1 tsp. coarse salt**
- **1 tsp. cayenne pepper**

1. Mix marinade ingredients in a bowl and pour over ribs which have been sliced into single ribs. Marinate in refrigerator for one hour.

2. Preheat gas grill for 10 minutes with burners on high.

3. Turn burners to medium and place ribs on grill reserving marinade. Close grill lid. Cook 10 minutes per side for well done. Remember, do not eat pink pork. Baste with marinade after turning. You may want to increase the flames to high for last two minutes to blacken meat.

Serves:

Hong Kong Spareribs

I've never been to China, but a native cook shared this recipe from the kitchen of his American restaurant. Seems I'd eaten so many spareribs at his buffet that he saved money by my eating at home instead. Just remember to have some napkins nearby. After all, we may be cavemen, but we're not Neanderthals!

6 pounds spareribs

Honey Sauce:
    1 cup honey
    1/2 cup soy sauce
    1/2 cup sesame seeds
    1 tbsp. brown sugar
    2 tsp. rice vinegar
    1 tsp. black pepper

1. Preheat gas grill for 10 minutes with burners on high.

2. Combine ingredients for sauce.

3. Turn burners to medium and place ribs on grill. Close grill lid. Baste with sauce after 3 minutes, continue cooking for 5 more minutes. Turn ribs and baste again after 3 minutes and cook for an additional 5 minutes. Remember, do not eat pink pork.

4. Remove ribs from grill, baste with remaining sauce and pour extra into side bowls for dipping.

Serves:

STUFFED PORK CHOPS

Sometimes, one meat just isn't enough for a hungry caveman. He wants pork and chicken or sausage or beef. If you can stuff a turkey, you can stuff a pork chop. Just buy the special thick ones!

6 (6 ounce) butterfly cut pork chops
12 ounces chicken filets
1/2 cup honey
2 tbsp. brown sugar
1/2 cup sesame seeds
1/2 cup barbecue sauce (see pages 13-15)

1. Preheat gas grill for 10 minutes with burners on high.

2. Wash chicken filets. Grill over high flames for 4 minutes per side. Leave grill lid open. Remove and return to preparation area.

3. Wash pork under cold running water and rinse out pocket. Combine honey, brown sugar and sesame seeds and coat chicken. Place chicken inside pocket of pork chop. Baste chop with barbecue sauce.

4. Turn burners to medium and leave grill lid open. Cook chops 6 minutes per side, basting with barbecue sauce after turning and again after removing from grill. Remember, do not eat pink pork.

Serves:

LAMB

ROAST
RACK OF LAMB

A popular Asian dish, many Americans haven't eaten lamb. But once you've tried lamb, beef and chicken will now have a third contender for your taste buds. When purchasing lamb, ask the butcher to remove the backbone so the ribs will peel away when done. Buy only "grown naturally" lamb that isn't injected with hormones, steroids and antibiotics!

Rack of lamb (10 to 18 ribs)

Basting Sauce:
>   **2 celery stalks, chopped**
>   **1 cup olive oil**
>   **1/4 cup chopped parsley**
>   **1/4 cup chopped onions**
>   **1/4 cup chopped carrots**
>   **1 tsp. black pepper**
>   **1 tsp. salt**
>   **dash of lemon juice**

1. Preheat gas grill for 10 minutes with burners on high.

2. In a bowl, combine ingredients for basting sauce.   Baste lamb before placing on grill.

3. Turn burners on one side of grill to low and place lamb over that area for indirect heating.   Close grill lid.

4. Cook for 1 1/2 hours.   Baste every 20 minutes.

Serves:

Mint Leg of Lamb

A real caveman food. Sitting around a fire, devouring a roasted leg of lamb in your hands; makes you want to howl at the moon!

4 (1 pound) legs of lamb

Mint Marinade:
    juice of 1 medium orange
    juice of 1 medium lemon
    2 tbsp. chopped mint
    1 tsp. olive oil
    1/2 tsp. ground pepper

1. Mix marinade ingredients in a bowl. Pour over lamb and marinate for 10 minutes in refrigerator.

2. Preheat gas grill for 10 minutes with burners on high.

3. Turn burners to medium and place lamb on grill reserving marinade. Close grill lid. Baste with marinade and cook 12 minutes per side, basting after turning.

Serves:

LAMB CHOPS

Americans may prefer beef, but lamb offers a tasty alternative!

8 (3 ounce) lamb chops

Marinade:
  1 small onion, diced
  1 small green bell pepper, diced
  1/4 cup olive oil
  1 tsp. lime juice
  1/2 tsp. ground pepper

1. Combine marinade ingredients in a small bowl. Pour over chops and marinate for 10 minutes in refrigerator.

2. Preheat gas grill for 10 minutes with burners on high.

3. Turn burners to medium and place chops on grill reserving marinade. Close grill lid. Cook for 8 minutes per side. Baste with marinade after turning.

Serves:

SHISH KABOBS

Arabic for "skewered meat," shish kabob was meant for lamb. By cutting lamb into sections and alternating it with several vegetables on skewers, you can have an entire meal from the grill. However, I suggest brown rice as a side dish.

> **2 pounds boneless leg of lamb**
> **3 medium onions**
> **1 large green bell pepper**
> **12 cherry tomatoes**
> **12 mushrooms**
> **juice of 1 medium lemon**
> **dash of black pepper**

1. Preheat gas grill for 10 minutes with burners on high.

2. While grill is heating, cut lamb into 2-inch chunks. Quarter onions and cut green bell pepper into 12 pieces.

3. Thread lamb and vegetables onto skewers (if using wooden skewers, soak for 20 minutes before using). Alternate lamb, tomato, bell pepper, mushroom and onion. Sprinkle with lemon juice and season with pepper.

4. Turn burners to medium. Place skewers on grill. Close grill lid. Cook 6 minutes per side.

Serves:

LEG OF LAMB

Cavemen love food they can eat with their hands.
This leg of lamb is pure nirvana!

4 (2 pound) legs of lamb (with bone)

Marinade:
    1 cup olive oil
    1/2 cup brown mustard
    2 tbsp. oregano
    1 tbsp. black pepper
    1 tbsp. minced onion

1. Combine marinade ingredients, pour over lamb and marinate for 30 minutes in refrigerator.

2. Preheat gas grill for 10 minutes with burners on high.

3. Turn burners to low. Place lamb on grill reserving marinade. Close grill lid. Grill 45 minutes for rare, 55 minutes for medium and 65 minutes for well done. Flip and baste with marinade midway and baste again 5 minutes before done.

Serves:

FISH & SEAFOOD

FRUIT SHRIMP KABOBS

Looking for a sweeter shrimp kabob? Your mouth will water from this Hawaiian recipe. It will really make you shake your grass skirt!

24 peeled large shrimp
3 medium apples
3 medium plums
3 medium oranges
24 (2-inch) pineapple cubes

1. Preheat gas grill for 10 minutes with burners on high.

2. Cut apples, plums and oranges into eighths. Alternate ingredients on four skewers (if using wooden skewers, soak for 20 minutes before using). Any combination is fine such as shrimp-pineapple-plum-orange-apple.

3. Turn burners to low. Place skewers on grill. Close grill lid. Cook for 6 minutes per side.

4. Remove and serve.

Serves:

BARBECUED SALMON

How about some salmon that bites back? Salmon is splendid if you merely put the fish on the grill, but the flavor comes alive with barbecue sauce!

4 (6 ounce) salmon fillets
Marinade:
　1/4 cup olive oil
　2 tbsp. Tabasco® sauce
　1 tbsp. dill
　1 tbsp. butter
　1 tsp. ground black pepper
juice of 1 lemon

1. Combine marinade ingredients in a bowl. Pour over fillets and marinate in refrigerator for 30 minutes.

2. Preheat gas grill for 10 minutes with burners on high.

3. Turn burners to medium and place fillets on grill reserving marinade. Spoon half of marinade over top. Close grill lid. Cook 6 minutes per side, basting with remaining marinade after turning.

4. Remove from grill and sprinkle with lemon juice.

Serves:

VEGETABLE SHRIMP KABOBS

The Conch Republic, also known as Key West, is a haven for shrimp lovers. Businessmen call it "Pink Gold" because tourists love the large shrimp from the Gulf of Mexico. They sound like Forrest Gump's friend, Bubba, when rattling off ways to make shrimp. This is a perfect combination of shrimp and vegetables that, combined with rice, makes a complete meal.

24 peeled large shrimp
3 small onions
3 medium green bell peppers
24 cherry tomatoes
1 cup barbecue sauce (see pages 13-15)
juice of 1 lemon

1. Preheat gas grill for 10 minutes with burners on high.

2. Cut onions and bell peppers into eighths. Alternate ingredients onto four skewers (if using wooden skewers, soak for 20 minutes before using). Any combination is fine such as shrimp-tomato-onion-pepper. Brush barbecue sauce on shrimp.

3. Turn burners to low. Place skewers on grill. Close grill lid. Cook 6 minutes per side, basting shrimp with barbecue sauce after turning.

4. Remove from skewers and sprinkle with lemon juice.

Serves:

GINGER SALMON

Cavemen have always loved a fish that literally jumps into their arms during spawning season. Salmon are among the tastier fish, very nutritious and the oils help arthritis sufferers. Legendary Celtic caveman Fionn MacCumhail was supposedly given unlimited wisdom when tasting salmon juice while it cooked. Consider it brain food!

4 (6 ounce) salmon fillets

Marinade:
    1 cup white wine
    1 tbsp. brown sugar
    1 tbsp. fresh ginger
    1 tsp. olive oil

juice of 1 lemon

1. Mix marinade ingredients in a bowl. Pour over fillets and marinate in refrigerator for 30 minutes.

2. Preheat gas grill for 10 minutes with burners on high.

3. Turn burners to medium and place fillets on grill. Spoon marinade on top. Close grill lid. Cook 6 minutes per side, basting with marinade after turning.

4. Remove from grill and sprinkle with lemon juice.

Serves:

GINGER SWORDFISH

Swordfish is one of the firmer fish meats. It's like eating a tender seafood steak.

4 (6 ounce) swordfish fillets

Marinade:
 1/4 cup lemon juice
 1 tbsp. ginger
 2 tsp. olive oil

salt and pepper to taste

1. Combine marinade ingredients in a bowl. Pour over fillets and marinate in refrigerator for 30 minutes.

2. Preheat gas grill for 10 minutes with burners on high. Spray grill with canola oil before lighting.

3. Turn burners to medium. Place fillets on grill reserving marinade and cook for 5 minutes. Close grill lid. Turn, baste with remaining marinade and cook for 5 minutes longer.

4. Place on a serving platter and season with salt and pepper.

Serves:

BARBECUED SWORDFISH

You may think you're eating a beef dish.
Swordfish is very tender, but doesn't fall apart on the grill.

4 (6 ounce) swordfish fillets

Marinade:
    2 tbsp. Tabasco® sauce
    1 tbsp. butter
    2 tsp. A-1® sauce
    1 tsp. ground black pepper

1. Combine marinade ingredients in a bowl. Pour over fillets and marinate in refrigerator for 30 minutes.

2. Preheat gas grill for 10 minutes with burners on high.

3. Turn burners to medium and place fillets on grill. Spoon half of the marinade over top. Close grill lid. Cook 6 minutes per side, brushing with remaining marinade after turning.

Serves:

BLACKENED SWORDFISH

This is an acquired taste, but those who love it will swear by it. I suspect some cavemen just overcooked their swordfish until it was burned, then said they meant to do that and ate it anyway!

4 (6 ounce) swordfish fillets

Basting Sauce:
    juice of 1 lemon
    2 tbsp. cayenne pepper
    2 tbsp. Tabasco® sauce

juice of 1 lemon
salt and pepper to taste

1. Preheat gas grill for 10 minutes with burners on high.

2. Combine basting sauce ingredients in a bowl. Baste fillets.

3. Know how I always say to lower the burners? Not this time. Leave them on high! Place fillets on grill. Leave grill lid open.

4. Cook 8 minutes per side, basting after turning. Like the name says, they should be black on both sides.

5. Sprinkle with lemon juice and season with salt and pepper.

Serves:

GRILLED FLOUNDER

The secret to cooking fish is preventing it from drying out. That's not easy on the grill. I don't use many dry rubs, but this one will retain the moist flavor.

4 (6 ounce) flounder fillets

Dry Rub:
2 tbsp. dry white wine
1 tbsp. dill
1 tbsp. paprika

juice of 1 lemon

1. Mix ingredients for rub. Wash and dry fish. Sprinkle rub onto fish and rub it in. Refrigerate for 30 minutes. Remove fillets, reserving rub mixture.

2. Preheat gas grill for 10 minutes with burners on high. Spray canola oil on grill before lighting.

3. Turn burners to medium. Place flounder on grill. Close grill lid. Cook for 5 minutes per side, applying more rub after turning.

4. Sprinkle with lemon juice when serving.

Serves:

SPICY CATFISH

A Southern caveman favorite for more than a century. Serve catfish with baked beans and cornbread and you won't be hungry again for days!

4 (6 ounce) catfish fillets (no whiskers, please)

Marinade:
- **1/2 cup olive oil**
- **1 tbsp. cayenne pepper**
- **1 tsp. black pepper**
- **1 tsp. Tabasco® sauce**

juice of 1 lemon

1. Combine marinade ingredients and pour over catfish. Marinate in refrigerator for 30 minutes.

2. Preheat gas grill for 10 minutes with burners on high. Spray canola oil on grill before lighting.

3. Turn burners to medium. Place catfish on grill reserving marinade. Close grill lid. Cook 5 minutes per side, brushing with marinade after turning.

4. Sprinkle with lemon juice when serving.

Serves:

Seasoned Lobster

Many cavemen never had the chance to try lobster, but those that did probably enjoyed it as much as I do!

4 (8 ounce) lobster tails (thawed)

Basting Sauce:
1 cup butter
juice of 2 lemons
2 tsp. Old Bay® seasoning
salt and pepper to taste

1. Preheat gas grill for 10 minutes with burners on high.

2. Wash tails and dry. Cut the bottom side of shell and crack shell partly open. Melt butter in a saucepan and add lemon juice and seasonings. Baste tail with mixture.

3. Turn burners on one side to low and place tails with split shell side down on grill. Leave other burner on high. Close grill lid and cook for 10 minutes.

4. Remove lobster meat from shell and serve with remaining basting sauce.

Serves:

SHARK STEAKS

Cavemen love to eat animals that could eat them. Really, how much fun is it to eat a cow when it's never going to eat you? But triumphing over a prey that could have eaten you is enough to make the caveman howl in victory!

4 (1-inch thick) shark steaks

Basting Sauce:
   2 tbsp. butter
   4 tbsp. lime juice
   1/2 tsp. black pepper

1. Preheat gas grill for 10 minutes with burners on high.

2. Melt butter and combine with lime juice and pepper. Baste shark steaks.

3. Turn burners to medium and place steaks on grill. Close grill lid. Cook 6 minutes per side, basting after turning.

Serves:

Swordfish Steaks

Swordfish is one of the easier seafoods to prepare, maybe because you don't need skewers. The meat is firm, yet succulent and filling. It makes a caveman want to grab his fishing pole!

4 (1-inch thick) swordfish steaks

Basting Sauce:
    2 tbsp. butter
    4 tbsp. lime juice
    1/2 tsp. black pepper

1. Preheat gas grill for 10 minutes with burners on high.

2. Melt butter and combine with lime juice and pepper. Baste swordfish steaks.

3. Turn burners to medium and place steaks on grill. Close grill lid. Cook 6 minutes per side, basting after turning.

Serves:

SMOKED MEATS

Smoked Chicken

Chicken is cooked more ways than any other meat. Smoked chicken takes a little longer to cook, but it's well worth the wait!

4 chicken breasts
4 chicken parts (legs, wings)

Basting Sauce:
1 cup barbecue sauce (see pages 13-15)
1 tbsp. ground black pepper
1 tsp. salt

1. Light your smoker.

2. Mix basting sauce ingredients in a bowl. Baste chicken, reserving remaining baste for later.

3. Place chicken inside smoker and cook 45 minutes, turning and basting once.

4. After removing from smoker, baste once more before serving.

Serves:

SMOKED HAM

Is there any part of the pig that we won't barbecue? You can grill ham on a gas grill, but it's much better in a smoker. Be sure to use maple chips as a sweetener!

1 (8 pound) ham
1 can (20 ounces) pineapple chunks, juice reserved

Basting Sauce:
  1 cup honey
  1/2 cup vegetable oil
  reserved pineapple juice

1. Light your smoker.

2. Trim fat from ham and wash thoroughly. Mix basting sauce ingredients in a bowl and baste ham with half of it.

3. Place ham on rack and close lid. Baste hourly for the next 4 hours. The rule of thumb is 30 minutes cooking time for every pound of ham. Don't forget to check the coals for consistent heat.

4. Check the meat thermometer. When it reads 180 degrees and the juices are clear, the ham should be done. I always recommend making a small incision to check for doneness.

5. After removing ham, place pineapple chunks on skewers and place on grill (if using wooden skewers, soak for 20 minutes before using). When you're done slicing the ham and ready to serve, retrieve pineapple and serve hot with ham.

Serves:

Flattened Turkey

The first time I saw someone make flattened turkey, I thought "Lord, it's bad enough we killed the poor bird, but do we have to beat the hell out of it, too?" The preparer didn't think it was funny, but still showed me an innovative and tasty way to make turkey. Try it once and you'll never put your mallet away!

1 (10 pound) turkey (defrost if frozen)

Basting Sauce:
 2 cups butter
 1/4 cup onion flakes
 1 tsp. salt
 1 tsp. black pepper

1. Light your smoker. Have coals hot before starting to cook turkey.

2. Place soaked wood chips of your choice on coals. I recommend the mesquite chips.

3. While coals are warming, wash turkey under cold running water and remove innards. Now here's the key—beat that bird to death! Using a large carving knife, cut the bird in half down the backbone while also removing legs. Now you have two big pieces of meat. Place each end with bone side down and start smacking it using a large wooden mallet. This prevents ripping the flesh. Keep going until it's . . . well, flat. Remove the bone. You now have a much flatter piece of bird that won't take as long to cook. Combine basting sauce ingredients, baste turkey and place it in the smoker.

4. The nice part of cooking a flattened turkey is the cooking time is only two-thirds that of a whole bird. That still means 4 hours. Baste turkey every hour and keep those coals hot!

Serves: 🗿🗿🗿🗿🗿🗿🗿🗿🗿🗿

Ten Things To Do While Smoking A Turkey

1. Drive from Washington to Philadelphia, ring the Liberty Bell and head back to the White House.

2. Run a marathon . . . backwards.

3. Watch an NFL double-header.

4. Cut your grass, your neighbor's grass, and well, probably the entire block's grass.

5. Call GEICO every 15 minutes for car insurance rates. That's 24 calls. Maybe they'll lower it just to stop you from calling and annoying them.

6. Eat lunch and dinner.

7. Watch the entire Ben-Hur movie.

8. Learn a foreign language. "El pavo es muy delicioso."

9. Have that relationship talk your girlfriend has always wanted. For married couples, discuss when you're going to have kids, or when you can plan your next vacation without them.

10. Cook other recipes on your gas grill. You should have enough food to feed all the neighbors who have been lured by the smell coming from your smoker.

JESSE'S SMOKED TURKEY

My brother-in-law, Jesse, is king of the smokers. It's not Thanksgiving without one of his smoked gobblers. Believe me, the Pilgrims never had it this good and neither have you!

1 (10 pound) turkey (defrost if frozen)

Basting Sauce:
1 cup butter
1/4 cup onion flakes
1 tsp. salt
1 tsp. black pepper

1. Light your smoker. Have coals hot before starting to cook turkey.

2. Place soaked wood chips of your choice on coals. I recommend mesquite, but it's your bird.

3. While coals are heating, wash turkey under cold running water and remove innards. Combine basting sauce ingredients. Brush turkey with baste and insert thermometer.

4. Place turkey on lower rack of smoker and close lid.

5. Get a life because this is going to take awhile. In fact, it could take 6 hours for a large turkey. Baste turkey and stir the coals every hour. Maintain ultimate heat during entire cooking time! (See *Ten Things To Do While Smoking A Turkey,* page 57.)

6. How do you know when it's finally done? The thermometer should read 165 degrees. The juices should run clear when turkey is poked by a fork. Finally, cut a little slice in the breast and check.

7. Remove turkey with two large forks to pan placed beside smoker. If you drop the bird, at least drop it in the pan.

Serves:

SMOKED LAMB

Lamb may be the meat best enhanced by smoking. The flavor seeps all the way to the bone. I'm telling you, it's not baaaaaaad!

4 (2 pound) legs of lamb (with bone)

Marinade:
6 ounces golden mustard
1 cup olive oil
2 tbsp. fresh basil
1 tbsp. fresh ground black pepper
1 tbsp. minced onion
1 tbsp. soy sauce

1. Light your smoker.

2. Combine marinade ingredients and pour over legs of lamb. Marinate in refrigerator for 30 minutes.

3. Place lamb on bottom rack of smoker reserving marinade. Cook 50 minutes for rare, 60 minutes for medium and 70 minutes for well done. Halfway through cooking time, turn and baste lamb with marinade. Baste again 5 minutes before removing from smoker.

Serves:

Smoked Salmon

Salmon is so firm you may think you're cooking beef. But salmon is much healthier and has its own distinct flavor. Smoking will preserve its beneficial oils, especially when using a dry rub.

4 (6 ounce) salmon steaks

Dry Rub:
    1/4 cup olive oil
    1 tbsp. dill
    1 tbsp. butter
    1 tsp. ground black pepper

juice of 1 lemon

1. Light your smoker.

2. Wash salmon steaks and pat dry. Combine rub ingredients and rub onto salmon. Refrigerate for 20 minutes.

3. Place salmon on top rack of smoker reserving rub. Cook 15-20 minutes per side, applying rub after turning.

4. Remove from smoker and sprinkle with lemon juice.

Serves:

SMOKED LEG OF VENISON

Cavemen can eat this with their hands and howl at the moon in triumph. Here's a simple recipe that doesn't mask venison's natural flavor.

1 (3 pound) boned leg of venison

Marinade:
1 small onion, chopped
1/2 cup olive oil
1/2 cup melted butter
1 tsp. pepper
1 tsp. salt

1. Light your smoker.

2. Mix all marinade ingredients in a large bowl and pour over venison. Marinate in refrigerator for 30 minutes.

3. Place venison on bottom rack of smoker reserving marinade. Cook 8 minutes per side for rare, 12 minutes for medium and 15 minutes for well done. Baste with marinade after turning.

Serves:

EXOTIC MEATS

MOOSE STEAKS

If you can shoot Bullwinkle and bring home the meat, then you are the head of the caveman clan because these magnificent animals could feed you for months!

4 (1 pound) moose steaks

Basting Sauce:
    1 cup melted butter
    1 tbsp. pepper
    1 tbsp. coarse salt

1. Preheat gas grill for 10 minutes with burners on high.

2. I'll keep this very simple. Combine basting sauce ingredients, pour half over steaks and throw them over a hot flame. Leave grill lid open. Cook 4 minutes per side and eat rare (or, at most, medium). Baste again with remaining sauce after turning.

Serves:

VENISON PICANTE KABOBS

Let's spice things up with a south of the border dish taught to me during a Latin-dish dinner with Peruvian friends. They could make wheat bread taste spicy!

2 pounds venison (any part)

Marinade:
- **2 ounces pimento**
- **3 tbsp. ketchup**
- **2 tbsp. chili flakes**
- **1 tbsp. Worcestershire sauce**
- **1 tbsp. mustard**
- **1 tbsp. pepper**
- **1 tsp. salt**
- **1 tsp. onion flakes**
- **1 tsp. A-1® sauce**
- **1 tsp. hot pepper sauce**

1 small bottle picante sauce

1. Cut venison into 2-inch cubes. Mix marinade ingredients in a bowl and pour over venison. Marinate in refrigerator for 30 minutes. Place meat on skewers and reserve marinade (if using wooden skewers, soak for 20 minutes before using).

2. Preheat gas grill for 10 minutes with burners on high.

3. Turn burners to medium and place skewers on grill. Close grill lid. Cook 3 minutes per side for rare, 5 minutes for medium and 7 minutes for well done. Baste with marinade after turning.

4. Remove venison from skewers and serve. Use picante sauce as a side dip.

Serves:

BARBECUED SQUIRREL

Squirrel hunting is a rite of passage for some young cavemen. Their elders figure they should start small and work their way up to something that either takes a lot of skill or is big enough to fight back. About the worst a squirrel can do is throw some acorns at cavemen after an errant shot!

2 squirrels

Marinade:
    2 cups barbecue sauce (see pages 13-15)
    1 cup water
    1 tsp. black pepper
    1 tsp. onion flakes
    1/2 tsp. salt
    1/2 tsp. thyme

1. Cut squirrels into 6-8 pieces. Combine marinade ingredients and pour over meat. Marinate in refrigerator for 30 minutes.

2. Preheat gas grill for 10 minutes with burners on high.

3. Turn burners to medium and place meat on grill reserving marinade. Leave grill lid open. Cook 5 minutes per side for rare, 8 minutes for medium and 10 minutes for well done. Baste with marinade after turning.

Serves:

STAY OPEN-MINDED & TRY SOMETHING NEW!

*You won't find most of these meats in your local supermarket. However, there are some good exotic meat companies on the Internet where you **can** get them.*

Rabbit Stew

This stew is dedicated to cartoon caveman Elmer Fudd, who never finished making it despite having Bugs in the pot countless times. (No, I don't have roadrunner stew elsewhere and dedicate it to Wiley Coyote). Rabbits vary per region of the country, but they all taste much like chicken. Don't tell your guests and they'll never know!

4 pounds rabbit filets (2 wascally wabbits)
1 gallon water
8 carrots, sliced
8 precooked whole potatoes, quartered
6 celery stalks, sliced
2 small onions, chopped
salt and pepper to taste

1. Preheat gas grill for 10 minutes with burners on high.

2. Fill cooking pot with water vegetables and seasoning and let boil on high flames on one side of grill.

3. Turn burners on other side of the grill to medium-low and place rabbit filets on it. Leave grill lid open. Cook 6 minutes per side for medium-to-well. Place rabbit in soup pot. Soup should boil for at least 15 minutes (or until carrots are tender).

4. Remove from heat and let thicken for 5 minutes. If needed, sprinkle in 1 cup of flour to thicken.

Serves:

BILLY GOAT GUMBO

The closest I've ever come to bagging a mountain goat was with my car when driving over the Rocky Mountains outside Denver and finding several goats on the road begging for food from kids who thought it would be cute to feed them from the car. I'm 14,000 feet up on a winding road with no guardrails and nearly go over the side to my death because kids and their parents are giving rolls to a goat. No wonder cavemen didn't really invent the wheel. Anyway, I wouldn't have minded preparing this recipe on the spot!

4 pounds goat meat (any part)
1 pound sausage
8 whole potatoes
3 small onions
2 gallons water
4 cups navy beans
4 cups brown rice
1/2 cup Worcestershire sauce
2 tsp. cayenne pepper

1. Light your smoker and gas grill. We're getting fancy.

2. Fill a large pot with non-meat ingredients and place in smoker.

3. Turn gas grill burners to medium and place goat and sausage on separate sides. Close grill lid. Sausage should be cooked 4 minutes per side, then sliced and added to gumbo. Goat should be cooked 8 minutes per side, sliced and added to gumbo.

4. Cook gumbo for 45 minutes. Let stand 10 minutes to thicken.

Serves:

BEAR & BEER STEAKS

Bear meat has always been a staple of the caveman's diet (and sometimes vice versa). Sometimes you might need a beer for courage to hunt bear, though I'd never advise trying it drunk. In fact, I buy bear meat from braver men than me and douse it in the champagne of blue-collar cavemen—beer!

3 pounds bear steaks,
1/2-inch cuts

Marinade:
2 (12 ounce) cans
dark beer
1 tbsp. ground pepper
1 tbsp. steak sauce
1 tsp. onion flakes
1 tsp. salt

1. Mix marinade ingredients and pour over bear steaks. Marinate in refrigerator for one hour.

2. Preheat gas grill for 10 minutes with burners on high.

3. Turn burners to medium and place steaks on grill reserving marinade. Close grill lid. Cook for 8 minutes per side. Baste with marinade after turning. Bear meat should always be served well done to avoid trichinosis. What's that? You don't want to know or chance getting it. Cook bear like you would pork to avoid food poisoning. That's why I suggest the thin cuts.

Serves: 🧑🧑🧑🧑

CHICKEN FAJITAS

Many Easterners have discovered this Southwestern staple in recent years at trendy restaurants. Caveman cooks can make this simple dish in minutes!

4 chicken breasts
8 tortillas
2 tomatoes, chopped
1 onion, chopped
2 cups shredded cheese
1 cup shredded lettuce

1. Preheat gas grill for 10 minutes with burners on high.

2. Debone chicken. Wrap tortillas in aluminum foil.

3. Turn burners to medium on one side and place chicken on grill. Turn other burners to low and place tortillas on grill. Close grill lid. Cook chicken for 5 minutes per side. Tortillas are just being heated.

4. Remove chicken and slice into strips. Place inside tortillas with other ingredients and wrap closed.

Serves:

CAVEMAN QUESADILLAS!

*Each recipe serves 4, but be prepared to make
4 more real soon!*

SAUSAGE & CHEESE

*Cavemen like tortillas on the grill for their burnt flavor. Cook the
sausage separately because tortillas don't last long on the grill!*

8 flour tortillas
1 cup chopped precooked sausage
3 cups shredded cheese
4 tbsp. butter

1. Preheat gas grill for 10 minutes with burners on high.
2. Lightly butter the outsides of all the tortillas. Which one is the outside? Have you been sniffing the propane? Pick a side!
3. Sprinkle cheese and sausage over top of 4 of the tortillas. Place another tortilla on top with the buttered side facing up.
4. Turn burners to low. Place tortillas on grill. Close grill lid.
5. After four minutes, flip tortillas using a spatula. Cook another three minutes with lid open.
6. Remove from grill and serve hot.

HAM & CHEESE

*I could call it grilled cheese sandwiches, but it sounds more
exotic this way. The biggest difference is using flour tortillas
instead of bread. Either way, these are delicious!*

8 flour tortillas
3 cups shredded cheese
1 cup chopped ham
4 tbsp. butter

1. Prepare and cook as per recipe above.

PIZZA

SEAFOOD PIZZA

Ahoy there, me cavemen. Here are plenty of toppings that are sure to give you a taste of the sea!

12-inch pizza dough or ready-made crust
4 ounces tomato sauce
4 ounces shredded mozzarella cheese
Toppings:
   1 cup precooked shrimp
   1/2 cup precooked crabmeat
   1/2 cup precooked lobster
   anchovies to taste

1. Preheat gas grill for 10 minutes with burners on high.

2. While grill is warming, prepare crust. A ready-made crust is fine, but you can make your own crust if you like. For those making their own crust, cook for 10 minutes at 400 degrees so dough rises without browning. Either crust should be placed on a 12-inch sheet pan. Be sure to measure your grill beforehand to ensure the pan fits with lid down.

3. Spread sauce with spatula. Cover with cheese. Add toppings.

4. Turn burners to medium. Place pan over grill and close grill lid.

5. Cook for 10 minutes or until cheese has melted.

Serves:

HAWAIIAN PIZZA

Aloha to boring pizza. I'm talking the sweetest pizza you've ever tasted!

12-inch pizza dough or ready-made crust
4 ounces tomato sauce

Toppings:
    6 ounces shredded mozzarella cheese
    6 ounces shredded precooked ham
    1 cup diced pineapple
    1 small orange, diced

1. Preheat gas grill for 10 minutes with burners on high.

2. While grill is warming, prepare crust. A ready-made crust is fine, but you can make your own crust if you like. For those making their own crust, cook for 10 minutes at 400 degrees so dough rises without browning. Either crust should be placed on a 12-inch sheet pan. Be sure to measure your grill beforehand to ensure the pan fits with lid down.

3. Spread tomato sauce with spatula. Cover with cheese and then ham, pineapple and orange. Mozzarella cheese works best with sweet toppings.

4. Turn burners to medium. Place pan on grill and close grill lid.

5. Cook for 10 minutes or until cheese has melted.

Serves:

CARNIVORE'S PIZZA

Pepperoni, sausage, ham, bacon—you're going to need two hands to eat this meatlover's pie!

12-inch pizza dough or ready-made crust
4 ounces barbecue sauce (see pages 13-15)

Toppings:
- **6 slices precooked bacon**
- **3 ounces precooked sausage**
- **3 ounces precooked ham**
- **2 ounces precooked pepperoni**
- **6 ounces shredded mozzarella cheese**

1. Preheat gas grill for 10 minutes with burners on high.

2. While grill is warming, prepare crust. A ready-made crust is fine, but you can make your own crust if you like. For those making their own crust, cook for 10 minutes at 400 degrees so dough rises without browning. Either crust should be placed on a 12-inch sheet pan. Be sure to measure your grill beforehand to ensure the pan fits with lid down.

3. Spread barbecue sauce with spatula. Slice all meats (trim fat from bacon) and place on pizza crust. Sprinkle cheese over all.

4. Turn burners to medium. Place pan on grill and close grill lid.

5. Cook for 10 minutes or until cheese has melted.

Serves:

THREE-ALARM PIZZA

*Chili isn't the only spicy dish you can make outdoors.
Make sure you have plenty of ice water or cold beer around
when eating this pizza!*

12-inch pizza dough or ready-made crust
4 ounces barbecue sauce (see pages 13-15)

Toppings:
    1/2 cup chopped green bell peppers
    1/2 cup chopped onions
    1/4 cup chopped black olives
    1/4 cup chopped jalapeño peppers
    1/4 cup chopped banana peppers

6 ounces shredded mozzarella cheese

1. Preheat gas grill for 10 minutes with burners on high.

2. While grill is warming, prepare crust. A ready-made crust is fine, but you can make your own crust if you like. For those making their own crust, cook for 10 minutes at 400 degrees so dough rises without browning. Either crust should be placed on a 12-inch sheet pan. Be sure to measure your grill beforehand to ensure the pan fits with lid down.

3. Spread barbecue sauce with spatula. Add toppings and sprinkle cheese over all.

4. Turn burners to medium. Place pan on grill and close grill lid.

5. Cook for 10 minutes or until cheese has melted.

Serves:

SIDE DISHES

CORN-ON-THE-COB

I learned this method while attending a Kentucky Derby party in Louisville. Some cavemen like to cook the corn while still in the husk while others wrap it in foil.

4 ears large fresh corn in husks
butter, salt and pepper

1. Preheat gas grill for 10 minutes with burners on high.

2. If you want to cook in husks, soak the corn for about 20 minutes before placing on grill. If cooked inside foil, shuck the corn and wash before wrapping.

3. Turn burners to low and place corn on grill. Close grill lid. It takes 20 to 25 minutes to cook either style. Turn after 10 minutes.

4. Remove corn from husks or foil. Season as desired with butter, salt and pepper. Serve hot.

SWEET POTATOES

When does a starch taste like dessert?
When it's sweetened on the grill!

4 medium sweet potatoes
butter to taste
4 tsp. sugar
2 tsp. cinnamon

1. Preheat gas grill for 10 minutes with burners on high.

2. While grill is warming, wash sweet potatoes and wrap in foil.

3. Turn burners on one side of grill to low and place sweet potatoes over it. Close grill lid. Potatoes will take about 40 minutes to cook. Flip every 20 minutes. They're ready when a knife cuts into them easily.

4. Remove from foil and split into halves horizontally. Spread with butter. When butter has melted, sprinkle each with 1 teaspoon sugar and 1/2 teaspoon cinnamon.

BAKED POTATOES

It's the same principle as cooking them in the oven,
but much tastier!

4 large potatoes
butter, salt and pepper

1. Preheat gas grill for 10 minutes with burners on high.

2. While grill is warming, wash potatoes and wrap in foil. This seals in the potato's natural sugar and makes the potato sweeter, plus prevents burning.

3. Turn burners on one side of grill to low and place potatoes over that side. Close grill lid. Cook 45 minutes, turning once. Potatoes are ready when easily penetrated by a knife.

4. Split and serve with butter, salt and pepper.

CAJUN CORN

Cajun cavemen love spicy food. Indeed, if you don't drink a half dozen glasses of ice water while eating their food, it's not spicy enough. Three-alarm chili is Kool-Aid to Cajuns. They gargle with hot sauce! Our advice on spices is start mild and work your way up.

4 large ears fresh corn in husks
butter, pepper and cajun spice

1. Preheat gas grill for 10 minutes with burners on high.

2. Shuck the corn. Butter lightly and sprinkle on pepper and cajun spice of your choice. Some use Old Bay® Seasoning which is also used on seafood. Wrap in foil.

3. Turn burners to medium and place corn on grill. Close grill lid. It takes 20 to 25 minutes to cook. Turn after 10 minutes. Serve.

BAKED BEANS

It's not a cookout without baked beans. Indeed, backyard barbecuers will argue over who makes the best baked beans just as vehemently as those who debate over who makes the best chili!

2 (40 ounce) cans baked beans (tomato based)
1 small onion, diced
6 ounces chopped ham
1 cup water
1/2 cup ketchup
1/2 cup brown sugar
2 tbsp. maple syrup
1 tbsp. barbecue sauce (see pages 13-15)
dash of pepper

1. Light your smoker and clear your calendar.

2. Combine all ingredients in a large cast-iron pot. Leave grill lid open. Let cook for two hours. Stir every 30 minutes.

Serves:

CAVEMAN CRISPY FRIES

Anybody can make baked potatoes on the grill. Let's go to Cooking 102 and try sliced potatoes caveman style!

4 medium potatoes
1 cup corn flakes
1/2 cup butter, melted
salt and pepper to taste

1. Preheat gas grill for 10 minutes with burners on high.

2. Wash potatoes in cold water. After drying, cut lengthwise into eighths. That means cut them in halves, then in halves again and again.

3. Finely crunch corn flakes and mix with melted butter.

4. Place potatoes in a large plastic bag. Pour in corn flake mixture and shake vigorously until all potatoes are coated.

5. Turn burners to low on one side of grill. Place potatoes over the lower heat. Close grill lid. Cook for 20 minutes, then flip with spatula. Cook for another 20 minutes.

6. Season with salt and pepper.

Serves:

BLACK BEANS & RICE

For cavemen wanting something a little heartier, here's a chance to use both your smoker and your grill. Black beans and rice will stick to your ribs!

> 1 pound dried black beans
> 1 gallon + 3 cups + 1/2 cup water
> 2 pounds brown rice
> 1/2 pound precooked bacon
> 2 stalks celery, chopped
> 1 small onion, chopped
> 1 tbsp. ground pepper

1. Light smoker.

2. Place beans and 1 gallon of water in a cast-iron pot and place in smoker. Cook 2 hours. Beans should be soft.

3. When beans are almost done, preheat gas grill with burners on high for 10 minutes.

4. Place a large pot or kettle on gas grill, add 3 cups of water and bring to a boil; add rice. Leave grill lid open. Cook for 14 minutes or until water is absorbed by rice.

5. Drain beans and then add rice and other ingredients to pot. Add 1/2 cup water and return pot to smoker for 30 minutes.

Serves:

HAM & BEAN SOUP

The perfect outdoor soup. Grilled ham mixed with beans provides a thick soup that makes a hearty meal!

1 (12 ounce) can bean soup
1 (2 ounce) slice ham
1/2 cup water

1. Preheat gas grill for 10 minutes with burners on high.
2. Turn burners to medium. Place ham on grill and cook for 3 minutes per side. Leave grill lid open.
3. Pour soup into a cast-iron skillet. Heat on grill beside ham.
4. Once ham has seared on both sides, cut into bite-size pieces and mix into soup. Add water. Heat until soup comes to a boil.

CORNBREAD

You won't be able to make enough cornbread when your friends try this recipe. Nothing completes a meal of barbecue and beans more than cornbread. Best yet, it's simple to make on your grill!

2 cups yellow cornmeal
1 (16 ounce) can cream style corn
1 1/2 tbsp. baking powder
1 tsp. salt
butter

1. Preheat gas grill for 10 minutes with burners on high.
2. Mix together all ingredients (except butter) in a bowl.
3. Pour into a cast-iron skillet or pie pan.
4. Turn burners to medium and cook cornbread for 25 minutes with grill lid closed. When golden brown, remove and smother with butter.

FRUITS

PINEAPPLE SPEARS

Grilled fresh pineapple is a treat, but don't let the thought of coring a pineapple scare you away. Pineapple from a can works just as well!

1 cored pineapple (or 8 ounces from can)
3 tbsp. butter or margarine
2 tsp. brown sugar

1. Preheat gas grill for 10 minutes with burners on high.

2. While grill is warming, cut the ends off the pineapple and remove core. Cut into slices that are 1-inch thick. (For those of you using canned pineapple, cut into 1-inch thick slices.)

3. Mix butter with brown sugar. Microwave for 20 seconds on High. Baste pineapple.

4. Place on wooden or metal skewers (if using wooden skewers, soak for 20 minutes before using).

5. Turn burners to low. Place skewers on grill and cook for 5 minutes. Close grill lid. Turn and cook for 3 minutes. Pineapple is ready when it just starts to brown.

6. Serve with main dish.

Serves:

Spicy Apples

Hot apples are often used as a side dish for ham and pork, but they're also great for desserts. Green or red? It doesn't matter, but a firm texture is preferred over soft.

4 medium apples

Basting Sauce:
   2 tbsp. sugar
   2 tsp. cinnamon
   3 tbsp. butter

1. Preheat gas grill for 10 minutes with burners on high.

2. While the grill's warming, mix the sugar, cinnamon and butter in a microwaveable dish and heat until butter has melted and sugar dissolved. It often takes 25 seconds on a high setting. Cut apples in half and remove cores and seeds. Peeling the apples is optional.

3. Turn burners to medium on one side and low on the other side. Baste apples and place over low heat, skin side down. Close grill lid.

4. After 4 minutes, turn apples. Cook for 2 minutes.

5. Remove from grill and serve in bowls. Pour remaining sauce on top.

Fruit Kabobs

Choose your favorite fruits because you can use them all. However, apples, pineapples, plums, bananas and pears work best.

1-inch chunks of fruit (apples, pineapple, pears, etc.)
1 tsp. sugar
1/2 cup water

1. Preheat gas grill for 10 minutes with burners on high.

2. Alternate fruits on skewers (if using wooden skewers, soak for 20 minutes before using).

3. Turn burners to low. Place skewers on burners. Close lid. Cook 4 minutes.

4. Turn skewers and cook for an additional 2 minutes.

5. Mix sugar with water. Place in a sprayer bottle. After removing fruit from grill, spray with sugar water to moisten.

6. Serve in bowls.

Banana Split

Grilling bananas intensifies their flavor so don't monkey around with them. They're quite a treat when used in a banana split!

4 ripe bananas
1 gallon ice cream
chocolate syrup

1. Preheat gas grill for 10 minutes with burners on high.

2. Cut unpeeled bananas lengthwise. Lay skin side down on grill.

3. Turn burners to medium. Close grill lid.

4. After 3 minutes, flip bananas using spatula. Cook 2 minutes.

5. Remove from grill. Scoop banana from skin and arrange on ice cream. Add chocolate syrup.

BREAKFAST

The smell of eggs and bacon frying over open flames has awakened many caveman campers. Indeed, most caveman meals are well-suited for breakfast. You can even go pick the nuts and berries if you like. I won't show you how to make toast and coffee (Boy Scouts can do that), but here are a few morning eye-openers. Most recipes are for one person because breakfast tends to be more of an individual meal than lunch or dinner.

EGGS & HAM

If you were cooking over a campfire, you could dice the ham and scramble all together. But, let's suppose your gas grill is nearby.

> **2 eggs**
> **1 slice ham**
> **salt and pepper**

1. Preheat gas grill for 10 minutes with burners on high.

2. Turn burners to medium. Lay ham on one side of grill. Close grill lid. Cook each side for 3 minutes.

3. Cook eggs in cast-iron skillet on other side of grill. I like my eggs scrambled, but it's your choice.

PANCAKES

I know, you figure I've lost my mind. How does the batter not fall through the grates? By using a piece of sheet metal or a very large griddle on top of the grill. Sure, you can cook them in a frying pan, but that usually means making one at a time or several silver dollars. Believe me, you won't be able to make enough to satisfy everyone even if you're just cooking for yourself!

2 cups ready-made pancake mix
1 cup water
honey or syrup
butter

1. Preheat gas grill for 10 minutes with burners on high. Place sheet metal on top of grill. Spray with nonstick cooking spray or oil.

2. Mix ready-made batter (or make your own if you want to) in bowl. It's better thick than thin. You can add berries or chocolate chips, if you like.

3. Turn burners to medium. Make sure temperature is right by dropping a couple drops of water on the sheet metal. If it sizzles, you're ready to go.

4. Pour pancake batter on grill. About the size of your fist for starters. You can make bigger ones with some experience.

5. When batter bubbles, flip with spatula. Work the corners first to ensure evenness.

6. You only want to flip once, but if the first side seems a little runny then go ahead and flip once more.

7. Serve with honey or syrup and butter.

Serves:

GARDEN OMELET

Like a little of everything in your omelet?
Well, empty your refrigerator into this one!

2 eggs, lightly beaten
1/4 cup shredded cheese
diced onion
diced green onions
diced tomato
diced mushrooms
dash of Tabasco® sauce

1. Preheat gas grill for 10 minutes with burners on high.

2. Pour eggs into a cast-iron skillet and cook until the bottom is slightly firm. Before turning, spread cheese, both kinds of onion, tomato and mushrooms evenly over top. Sprinkle with Tabasco. I don't give exact measurements for the contents because most people tend to use their hands when adding them. It's more of a feel thing.

3. Using a spatula, fold the omelet in half, cook for 2 minutes and then flip over and cook for another 2 minutes.

Serves:

Steak & Eggs

The breakfast of champions. There's enough protein here to sustain a professional athlete, so you should zip through all of your morning tasks!

1 (12 ounce) T-bone steak
2 eggs
salt and pepper to taste

1. Preheat gas grill for 10 minutes with burners on high.

2. Salt and pepper steak before placing on grill. Turn burners to medium. Close grill lid. Cook steak 6 minutes per side.

3. Cook eggs in a cast-iron skillet. Add salt and pepper while frying or scrambling.

Serves:

Ham & Cheese Omelet

It doesn't take some snobby foreign caveman in a round white hat to make an omelet. It's one of the simplest of meals!

3 eggs, lightly beaten
3/4 cup shredded sharp cheese
1/2 cup chopped ham

1. Preheat gas grill for 10 minutes with burners on high.

2. Turn burners to medium. Cook eggs for 2 minutes in a cast-iron skillet. Before turning, spread cheese and ham evenly over top.

3. Using a spatula, fold the omelet in half, cook for 2 minutes and then flip over and cook for another 2 minutes.

Serves:

LUNCHTIME

GRILLED PB & J'S

That's right! PB&J on the grill! Your kids will love them. You'll end up eating two yourself. It's just a new twist on something we've all eaten a million times!

8 slices bread
peanut butter
jelly
butter

1. Preheat gas grill for 10 minutes with burners on high.

2. Make 4 peanut butter-and-jelly sandwiches. Lightly butter outsides of sandwiches.

3. Turn burners to medium. Place sandwiches on grill and toast for 3 minutes. Leave grill lid open. Flip and cook other side for 3 minutes.

Serves:

GRILLED CHEESE

Imagine yourself on a picnic in France. You've opened the wine, unwrapped the bread and sliced the cheese. Sounds nice, but let's jazz it up a little. Hopefully, there's a grill around!

1 large loaf French bread
1/2 pound sliced cheese
2 tsp. olive oil
2 tsp. butter

1. Preheat gas grill for 10 minutes with burners on high.
2. Slice the bread in half lengthwise. Spread butter across sliced inside areas. Baste outside of bread with olive oil. Put sliced cheese inside loaf and secure vertically with skewers.
3. Turn burners to low on one side of grill and place loaf on the low heat side. Close lid and cook for 8 minutes.
4. Remove from grill and slice into sandwiches.

TURKEY SAUSAGE DOGS

This healthy alternative has the great taste of sausage despite being made from turkey. It may confuse some cavemen so just say it's sausage. They'll smile, eat and enjoy!

1 pound turkey sausage
mustard
ketchup
4 hot dog buns

1. Preheat gas grill for 10 minutes with burners on high.
2. Slice turkey sausage lengthwise.
3. Turn burners to medium and place sausage on grill with sliced side facing down. Like hot dogs, there is no rare or well done. You're basically just heating them. Heating 3 minutes per side, with grill lid open, should be enough.

Grilled Ham & Cheese

Here we're just taking your traditional grilled cheese and going one step further.

1 large loaf French bread
1/2 pound sliced cheese
1/2 pound sliced ham
2 tsp. olive oil
2 tsp. butter

1. Preheat gas grill for 10 minutes with burners on high.
2. Slice the bread in half lengthwise. Spread butter across sliced inside areas. Baste outside of bread with olive oil. Put sliced cheese and ham inside loaf and secure vertically with skewers.
3. Turn burners to low on one side of grill and place loaf on the low heat side. Close grill lid and cook for 8 minutes.
4. Remove and slice into sandwiches.

Spamtastic

This "mystery meat" is mighty tasty when grilled and served as a burger!

7 ounces Spam®
A-1® sauce
2 slices cheese
2 burger buns

1. Preheat gas grill for 10 minutes with burners on high.
2. Turn burners to medium. Slice Spam lengthwise into 4 pieces.
3. Place on grill and cook for 3 minutes per side or until spam is thoroughly seared. Leave grill lid open.
4. Add A-1 sauce on top, then cheese for final minute of cooking.
5. Serve on buns.

Rick Snider is an award-winning journalist, author of seven books and president of 21st Century Online Publishing. He has covered professional sports for *The Washington Times* since 1985.

Snider's books cover health, sports and humor. He also spent three years as a broiler chef in a steakhouse. Snider lives in Waldorf, Maryland with his wife Lisa, daughters Megan and Katie and recipe-tasting dog Roxie.

INDEX

INDEX (continued)

ORDER BLANK

GOLDEN WEST PUBLISHERS

☼ 4113 N. Longview Ave. • Phoenix, AZ 85014

www.goldenwestpublishers.com • **1-800-658-5830** • FAX 602-279-6901

Qty	Title	Price	Amount
	Arizona Cook Book	6.95	
	Berry Lovers Cook Book	6.95	
	Best Barbecue Recipes	6.95	
	Chili-Lovers' Cook Book	6.95	
	Easy RV Recipes	6.95	
	Easy Recipes for Wild Game and Fish	6.95	
	Kansas Cook Book	6.95	
	Michigan Cook Book	6.95	
	North Carolina Cook Book	6.95	
	Recipes for a Healthy Lifestyle	6.95	
	Salsa Lovers Cook Book	6.95	
	Seafood Lovers Cook Book	6.95	
	Secrets of Caveman Cooking	6.95	
	Take This Chile and Stuff It!	6.95	
	Tequila Cook Book	7.95	
	Texas Cook Book	6.95	
	Tortilla Lovers Cook Book	6.95	
	Veggie Lovers Cook Book	6.95	
	Virginia Cook Book	6.95	
	Wisconsin Cook Book	6.95	

Shipping & Handling Add: United States $3.00
Canada & Mexico $5.00—All others $12.00

☐ My Check or Money Order Enclosed

☐ MasterCard ☐ VISA ($20 credit card minimum)

Total $ _____

(Payable in U.S. funds)

Acct. No. _____ Exp. Date _____

Signature _____

Name _____ Phone _____

Address _____

City/State/Zip _____

Call for a FREE catalog of all of our titles

5/02   **This order blank may be photocopied**   Secrets Caveman